# Journal

## of the

# First Step

# Journal
## of the
# First Step

Michael Heald

PUNCHER & WATTMANN

First published in 2022
Published by Puncher and Wattmann
PO Box 279
Waratah NSW 2298

https://www.puncherandwattmann.com
web@puncherandwattmann.com

ISBN    9781922571281

Cover design by David Musgrave
Typesetting by Morgan Arnett
Printed by Lightning Source International

NATIONAL LIBRARY OF AUSTRALIA

A catalogue record for this book is available from the National Library of Australia

I

# CHILD OF MATTER

Heir to that concept,

what you saw
and what you felt
as really there,
or let blur, dissolve
and looked straight through,
reached straight through,

was chosen for you
by its lens,
its nerve,

and so you appeared to yourself
in that world of appearances,
grew solid to yourself
in that world of solidities,

and continued, then,
the separating
of your so-called body,
and your so-called mind,
from the others,

until you were sure
you had distinguished
entirely the creature
you are,
and walked its world
capably, knowingly,

the teachers approving,
rulers rewarding,

and the elders
blessing the achievement
of your isolate prowl:

and so the first step
of a maturity that is your birthright
was never conceived of,
let alone attempted,
let alone taken.


## Disfigured

For the whole of my life so far
it has looked as if
I have a body
outside of me:

like a hairy wart
drooping from my mind:

rather than there being
this play
of colours and contours
wholly within it..

# The Fire

*O sages standing in God's holy fire*
*As in the gold mosaic of a wall,*
*Come from the holy fire, perne in a gyre,*
*And be the singing-masters of my soul.*

– WB Yeats, 'Sailing to Byzantium'

The sages cannot step
from the holy fire
because it is everything everywhere,
including them,

and your corporeal decay
and attendant melancholy –
desire-sick heart, dying animal and all –
are already shimmering
in the gold mosaic.

Our every moment is consumed
as it's born, yes,

but in what air
is it burning?

# II
# THE SO-CALLED BODY
## *Sensations*

# 1. Temptation

Each time one is felt
you are tempted
to believe
there is such a thing
as the body:

to fall.

# 2. Taking Its Measure

At first it feels like trying
to get the whole universe
into your frame of vision:

how could you ever step back far enough
to see its wavering edges touching
what it's not, and where
would you be then?

Not until you feel the sensation
happening without you

do you realise how
a vantage point may arise.

## 3. Seen

Seen one,
seen them all:

seen everything.


## 4. Netti Netti (Not This, Not That)

Your unpleasantness is not unhappiness
and your pleasantness not happiness.

Attraction to you is not need,
and aversion to you not discernment.

Your intensity is not urgency,
your magnitude not significance,
your duration not solidity.

And nor are your fluctuations
actual change.


## 5. Flames, or Ice-fronds

You can't tell:

the flames, or ice-fronds
pose ornately
as whichever you think
they are...

## 6. Everywhere

Somewhere in the sensation
is your craving for it,
or your hatred of it;

and somewhere in the sensation
is your belief
that it is brute reality;

and somewhere in the sensation
moves the story
in which you are always
the main character.

But everywhere
the sensation
is nothing
but knowing.


## 7. Fantasy

From the pleasantness
or the unpleasantness,
a story takes life...

Sensation:

fantasy's
very breath.

## 8. Marrow

How your opinions
first began to flow:

marrow
of your bony attitudes.


## 9. Pressure Point

The separate self's
pressure point,

to take it down.


## 10. Equanimity's Witness

You had only ever known them in captivity,
in the cage of reaction, on display
as the languid much-loved *pleasure,*
or the raging much-feared *pain,*

but now, like a naturalist in a hide,
you observe them in their element,

their movements neither
towards nor away from you,
neither threatening nor endearing,

and as you try to focus,
all you seem to see
are over-lapping shadows:

are you watching, remembering,
or imagining? Have you ever
really witnessed
those legendary creatures?


## 11. Creature

Such a flimsy ghost, the creature of reaction,
spun out of one brief sensation, one

haphazardly-thrown little shadow of yourself
that would have flickered past had you not
crouched in it, kept to its darkness;

one tiny spark which would never
have become that bushfire
had you not sheltered it,
fed it...


## 12. Opportunity

You can see it now,

the way that particular sensation
has enveloped you, over and over,
in a darkness from which
you only emerge
having made the same mistake.

Yet now it shimmers
as radiant opportunity.

## 13. The Infinite

Habitual evocations
of contact,
of solidity,
dispelled:

to feel them now is like

brushing up against
the infinite


## 14. Objecthood

Embarking on the scrutiny
of sensations,
I had only expected,
at most,
those

to waver
in front of my
closed eyes,

not all objects
with my eyes wide open:

objecthood itself, it turns out,
is a felt thing.

## 15. Ache

All of our suffering
is referred pain
from the aching clench of self.


## 16. Stone

Stone
has a bad name:

hard, lifeless, heavy, cold...

But as I sat, the warm fluidity
of my face
cooled and stilled, as if
turned to stone,

and the extension
of my body − the placing
of my hands, and feet,
at a distance from my trunk,
the lifting
of my head above it −
seemed all the work
of stone,

as if it was only just
occurring to creation
to form me in this way,

and it was not
a hardening or a deadening,
a sinking or a growing cold. No,
it was sheer coherence, both
a towering and a founding:

the intensest solidity
and the purest emptiness.

And I raised my crystalline eyes
to the stones of the earth
and saw how massively
we have misconstrued them.


## 17. Inflections of Nothingness

Sensation
evokes contact,

which implies solidity,

which suggests objects.

But search
the sensation again
for any of those things

and all you find are
inflections of nothingness...

## 18. Presence (Addendum)

The way you can feel your body
though it is not being touched:

like the hand of existence
resting on you:

resting *as you.*

## 19. Inside Out

As you watch for them,
and they reveal themselves,
you begin to feel
you're turning inside out,

then realise, no,
it was the way you were
first unfolded to yourself

that was the wrong way round,

that has left you, now,
slowly struggling out
of a skin-tight, back-to-front ontology.

# III
# THE DREAM-STRUGGLE

## The Step Towards Yourself

*You cannot stand up and take a step towards yourself.*
– Rupert Spira

And yet
there is a path…


## Dream-Struggle

You can't struggle free,

can't even
seem to
try properly,

then wake to yourself
in a posture of effortless passage
like Hermes mid-stride.


## Cell

A row of tiny rooms along the side
of the main hall, they remind me
of the wasps' nests at home:
solitary, body-fitted dwellings
on but not in the house.

Like PO boxes via which
you're to deliver
yourself to your Self,

or safety deposit from which
you hope to collect
something precious you already have
but haven't been able to access.

Absolutely nothing inside,
blandest of waiting rooms
for the appointment you're not sure
you've got with a different you...

As you close the flimsy door it seems
there's barely room to breathe.
You feel like a performance artist:
'man locked in
*moments that can't improve*
or can they?'

Or someone lured from the credulous audience
to be sealed in the magician's cabinet
and have the gleaming blades
of this world's suffering —
boredom, discomfort, loneliness —
passed clean through...

You sit
as if sat in the corner
for misbehaving,

as if sat
where the teacher can see you,

sat
to take a good hard look at yourself.

But your task is not merely to stay
in here, but in *now*, and you

just can't seem to do it —
this cell can't hold you,
you keep discovering yourself
at large in the past or the future,
and must drag yourself
sheepishly back, *smilingly*,
as instructed, but in fact despairing
of ever getting traction
on this frictionless terrain
called attention, of ever being alert
in the moment of drift
into remembering, imagining...

And so this is your
appointed struggle,
though hard to say what wheel it is
you've put your shoulder to,
which door you're pushing at
or trying to hold closed;

this is your house now,
whose only window
is onto the bodymind's dark.


Posture

After several whole
days like that, when
I lay down to sleep

it felt like I'd merely
toppled over in the
sitting position —

like one of those stone figures
outside an abandoned temple
that vines have drawn down —

as if posture is mental,
persisting like attitude.

## Sitting

When I'm sitting, my body
leans, sags, straightens, bows again
like a flame searching languidly
for its vanishing point.

## Jaw

Once, in my cell, my jaw
began to shiver: I thought
I might be about to speak
in tongues, babble prophecies,
but no words came,
only this teeth-chattering
without cold. Afterwards,

my friend told me his reiki teacher
had one day suddenly struck
his jaw, and he didn't stop crying

like a baby for hours, not from pain,
but because of all the stress
we store there suddenly released and flowing:

in my case the cathartic uppercut
must have been delivered
by the brawny marauding solitude
in any one of the numberless unguarded
moments of contemplation, the tension

juddering out in silent mouthings
like the Way's mimicry
of all the talk we drown it out
and misrepresent it with.


## Returning

Returning, I felt
as still as the proverbial mountain,
with everyone fidgeting
and chattering and darting
around me like birds.


## Creature of Habit

*Habits are breaking me...*
– Powderfinger

I'll wake, now, to find my attention
making its own way through the body, feeling
the sensations yieldingly, curiously, that

tightening of the heart to brace against or
grip not happening, as if the new habit
is up and running, the old one laid to rest.


## The Extrapolations

*...or to bring an oil lamp into a dark place,*
*So that those with eyes could see what was there...'...*

Sensations seem to form
a body,

thoughts seem to form
a mind,

perceptions seem to form
a world...

But when the lamp is brought

these extrapolations
gleam in the air for a moment —

gigantic arcane edifices — before

vanishing as utterly
as the darkness.

## The Profound Cheekiness of All Things

The profound cheekiness of all things,
their sheer larrikin affront to nothingness,
is lost on us now, so sunk as we are
into sombre credulity
by the dead weight of materialism's
belief in solidity,
in separateness.


## Purification

I know you'll be against
this word: I am, too.
Or was.

There are good reasons
to be against it, as a quick glance
at the twentieth, or any other
human century will show.

But when you feel
the poisons begin to leave you —
the anger, the lethargy, the despair —

not like moods that could at any time
return, but as if what you're made of
is changing for the better —

there is no other word for it.

# Time's Arrow

*...the distinction between the past, the present and the future is only a stubbornly persistent illusion.*
– Albert Einstein

Having heard it's possible, I sit
trying to feel my way back

through discomfort to what
sensation is before reaction,

the unyieldingness of the earth
pressing ache through my body, when

suddenly they disengage,
the ground's solidity is now just itself,

as is the tumultuous heat of my bones:
as if each has been taken

in the hand of its own concept
and drawn apart, showing me how

different facets of the diaphonous
sensation have been imbued

with significance, with character,
isolated and animated, by ideas –

the solidity by *perpetrator*
so it seems to inflict;

the heat by *victim*
so it seems to burn –

staging the melodrama
of those two stock actors...

But as I look from one
to the other I realise

only one can be experienced
at a time, because I am not

encountering, but performing them,
they are not entities, but actions

of the mind – fearing, self-pitying –
that swiftly alternate: they never

even coexist, let alone interlock...
And so as my suffering lies

dismantled in this weird peace,
the tick-tock of that impact

stopped; as those imagined
adversaries pixelate and mingle

back into the sensation-moment's
one coruscation, one ethereal flesh,

it feels like a great wound
is closing: as if time's arrow

is being drawn from my heart.

# Brink

The body
dissolves yet
remains, more
ethereally tangible,
weighing in
on different scales,

as if a new unsureness of the ground
were firming underfoot,

each experience like stepping
on a threshold, as if a massive

brink were accumulating, over which
I am destined to plunge...

# The Collapsings

Days that had felt so knotted,
so tearing: but afterwards,
their every event flowed
past as an unfelt stream
of arisings and collapsings,
going nowhere, a flickering stasis,

each step melting
as it pressed,

each emotion dissipating
as it gathered,

each attitude falling apart
as it went to take aim:

nothing could outlast
the instant of its formation.


# Reactive

### 1. *The Idiot*

The idiot of reaction
is what I have been:

shoved back and forth,
limp victim, between
the bullies
pleasure and pain.

### 2. *The Blind Worm*

Lunging and recoiling along...


# Kernel

One by one I'm stripping the husk
of reaction from each encounter,

but can't quite seem to taste
the kernel
of unhated, uncraved

experience left
resting on my tongue.


## Me In the Garden

Warmed, bright
and lively now, near midday,

after the hunching
and bracing against
a cool and breezy,
overcast Spring morning,

but untransformed:

still straining
away from discomfort
towards pleasure;

still wrestling the web
of attraction and repulsion
with death creeping closer;

not blossomed into peace, but
only my shrivelling face
with a streak of sun
smeared on it
by a passing moment.

# Gone

My heart was gone.

And my mind.

Those aching cores
of the feeling-self
and the thinking-self,

that are normally
always straining
as if it is they
who have to haul up
the feelings,
the thoughts,

and bear them along.

Yet the emptiness left,
the space
of effortlessness,
still glittered
with feelings
and thoughts.

The source from which
the moments of my existence
emanated was no longer
within me, and I felt

like one of those figures
humbled and rapt
as they are found by rays
of light that seem to shine


from their adoration's
vanishing point.


## If you start to look…

If you start to look
in your experience,
rather than in your thought,

you'll be unable to find things
you've always been sure of,

and begin to find things
you have dismissed as unreal.

Pain, for example, pixelates
into grains of innocuous sensation
dissolving as they arise,

and your 'self' keeps
flipping over out of reach
like a dropped ticket
on the blowy street.

And could that have been
a stand-alone happiness
beyond the turmoil of desire
you just felt:

could that have been
'peace'?


## Shell

Persisting in the belief
that thought is taking place
inside your head
is like remaining
the child that you were
when you believed the ocean
was inside the shell, because

a grown-up said it was and then
you seemed to hear it there.


## Equally Dreamt

Can you feel how
the heaviness of your own body
and the weightlessness of those
you see out there, balance
the dream-scales perfectly?

# Seeing

*All objects are made of seeing.*
– Rupert Spira

Your reasoning, now prepared
to get its hands dirty
in experience, unearths
what you'd assumed to be
the root of seeing –

an electrical tendril sent
down by the object
via light-ray,
through eyeball,
to draw on the fertile dark
of the brain so it blossoms
instantly in our awareness –

and asks: how is this not
merely seeing's own display,
juxtaposed images
masquerading as 'process',
sight pretending
to be insight?

You had never dug down
below the seen at all,

never held up
an answer,

only flourished
a florid restatement
of the question.


## Aftershock

Now that collision
has been avoided at the core,
you are shaken

by the touch of a massive
stillness.


## Clinging

I almost drowned once
from clinging to the ski rope
after falling, the onslaught
of salt-water ferocious
and unrelenting...

A gurgly, distant yelling
eventually got through —

let go!

The onslaught vanished
and I reclined buoyantly
with my long wooden feet up,
sleek and shining,

and down —
wobbly and dim —

savouring the salty
air.


## The Birds

When the birds
pass overhead
they are random,
puzzling, and you are
losing them somewhere,

like your life.

The strain of reaching
for what seems separate
aches in your every attempt
to understand,
to keep.

But the birds
did not arrive, and
nor did they leave:

they are your own being
as it plays in the sky
of infinite freedom.

# City

A blaze of forms
desire has created
appearing to consume
the pure space of formlessness;

a smoke of names,
dense and sharp,
appearing to darken
the pure light of knowing.

# Body

How do you stand
when the rug of the body
is pulled from under you?

# Situation

Its structure had revealed itself,
you thought: its character
had shone out...

but going back over it now,
after your reaction and
all of the reactions to that,
you find the crystal clarity you saw
was no more than a bleary gleaming,
the worn-shiny corner
of your preconception,

blinding you to other contours,
other dimensions,

until you'd blundered in
and they were revealed
by the damage you'd done.


## Love and Metaphor

As the prophets concoct
gorgeously impossible things
out of language's stock
of thing-names, rich jokes
supposed to make us realise
all things are make-believe,

most
don't get it, see only
the gorgeously
impossible things —

burning bushes, flying horses,
an ark bulging with all the creatures
afloat on the flooded world,
a corpse up and walking again —

and are filled with contempt,
silly wonder, or a terrible greed.

We must teach one another
about metaphor, or die.

## What Cannot Be Said

*Detachment,*
*emptiness,*
*non-self...*

Is it any wonder there is rejection, ridicule,
in a culture addicted to language,
when all that language can do
is say, no, no, but then
can't go on...


## The One Who Suffers

*There are moods in which we court suffering, in the hope that here, at*
*least, we shall find reality, sharp peaks and edges of truth. But it turns*
*out to be scene-painting and counterfeit.*
− Henry David Thoreau

Even when you feel
hurt at the core, and tears
begin a watery exploration
of the face, it is still as if
you are grieving for a character
not quite you, who you must
hold there, to be hurt.

## Splitting the Atom of Emotion

What is left
of your emotion
when the thought
is disentangled
from the sensation?

A frail pressure,
slight warmth,
hint of cold,
rumour of agitation.

Splitting the atom of emotion,
suffering implodes.


## Thought's Progress

like rain-trickles on a window
shifting jerkily
through shapes we seem
to recognize...


## Waking on the Train

Waking events seemed
to have continued, but then I woke —

a strip of sunlight was lying
slant-wise across the dry paddocks,
and some fluffy grey clouds

we're gliding fast and low
more or less towards us —

and I couldn't tell
which way I was heading:
was this the scene of the beginning
or the end of my working day?

Facing away from the direction of travel,
trees appeared and shrank away, but
was an embryonic city growing on the horizon
behind me, or would I soon be swallowed
backwards by the gaping outer suburbs
of my regional home town? The knowledge

at first seemed secure and to have merely
receded intact, but as I tried to make the forms
I knew fit the landscape as it flowed
at various speeds and shape-shifted alongside,
tried in vain to see in broad daylight
where I was, and to place myself
back in situations of the day so far,

it began to feel less and less
like waking further and more like trying
to re-start the dream that had been
interrupted by the other dream.

## The Golden Thread

A string of your actions
begins to glow,
to shine,
as you realise
it has led you,
and always will,
out of the labyrinth
of confusion and suffering.

The golden thread
isn't fairy-tale.


## Horizon

I brought one hazy
desire into focus,
one blurry promise
of future pleasure,

and watched
it dissolve: then felt

the entire horizon waver,
*towards* stall…

## The First Step

Thoughts loud and bustling:

then the decision felt
like a pushing off
in that direction,
as if there was
a landscape with me in it
and a destination towards which
I was now to stride, when

both push and
ground just

gave, leaving

only an airy shifting
here, a re-balancing afloat

like a cloud-curl, as if
the noise of solidity

had suddenly stopped,
dissolving location.

IV

THE OUTER WORKINGS

OF STILLNESS

# The Outer Workings of Stillness

*Powerful constituencies congratulate themselves on having escaped*
*into science, especially proselytizing atheists, philosophical critics of*
*traditional understandings of 'consciousness', neuroscientists dazzled*
*by the chemical and electrical activity in the brain (which some of*
*them mistake for thought), and enthusiasts for 'artificial intelligence'*
*who favour a model of mind-as-machine formerly popularized by*
*eighteenth-and early nineteenth-century materialists.*
— Felipe Fernández-Armesto

An abiding peace, beyond analysis,
becomes a risible delusion
in an age that thinks it has stepped
once and for all out of
an immature confusion
in which such mirages were believed:

on this side of the glowing threshold,
a saner light reveals everything
to be in unconscious motion,
including the ball of our own ground,
spinning and looping
in stressed-out circles.

But if you've ever felt
the exertions and travellings
of your own life —
the lungings towards
and veerings away from —
wind back in
to your knowing of yourself,
it might occur to you

that what is actually being witnessed
is not pervasive agitation
but the outer workings of stillness.


## Things

watch you bemusedly
as you go about
your reactions:
as you grab for them,
or flare up at them:

their very form
is the smile at your ignorance.


## The Kill

It's hard to watch as the lion,
with its loping run, springs
and clutches the antelope,

but the process from there,
which you'd imagined
desperate and chaotic
in fact looks rather orderly,
like a smooth changing
down through nature's gears,

life not so much torn up
as folding neatly into death:

even last attempts at escape,
kicks or writhings, don't amount
to frenzy, more like a disinterested
testing of what's possible,
before they end strangely soon
in the stillness of acceptance.

And the eating which follows
seems unhurried, a contemplative
receiving rather than ravaging:

The whole thing has the poise
and grace, in fact, of ceremony.


## Land Grab

*By the end of the 1840's, squatters had seized nearly twenty million
hectares of the most productive and best-watered Aboriginal
homelands, comprising most of the grasslands in what are now
Victoria, New South Wales, South Australia and southern Queensland.
It was 'one of the fastest land occupations in the history of empires.'*
— James Boyce

2016 and here I stand, here my house stands,
and my son-grown-tall, in Ballarat,
in the aftermath, on the ground-almost-zero
of colonial impact, the last stands of *Swampy Riparian,*
*Herb-rich Foothill,* and *Plains Grassy Woodlands*
huddled along rail tracks and roads,
or captive in the deserts of private property
with a knife at their throat.

The imperial grip might seem to have
relaxed a little, to let some earth
trickle through — as Whitlam's did
for Vincent's bemused hand to receive,
like an aged dark bowl-less Oliver,
the smile of his strong lips infinitely
more enigmatic than the Mona Lisa's —

so that grains of ancient sovereignties
start to speckle and colour in
the vast blanks of our maps, and new
legal terms are formed, squiffy as a CAPTCHA
with evasive remorse.

But have we grasped yet that *country*
has eluded us, that our attempts to shoot,
poison, chop or plough our way
to custodianship have failed,
that signing documents of our own composing
to confer ownership on ourselves
has signified nothing? We still behave as if
we have this place in our keeping,
withholding or dispensing concessions,

even as our blind clench
chokes, withers, and delivers it
to the delinquent flames…

Yet here am I, far
from where I was born, far even
from where I was first set down
on this massive island to resume
my dazzled, disoriented childhood,
swearing I get it, and that what I see here

is not *remnant native flora and fauna* loafing
like the neo-liberals' undeserving unemployed
in an otherwise *improved, productive* landscape,

but a kind of constancy being enacted:
as if the strange (to me) beauty I witness,
each shape and sound and motion,
is the country's keeping faith
with the primordial care and knowing
it's been torn from —

the blackwood's leafage radiating,
the green comb spider orchid's angel floating,
the snake wattle's yellow softly bustling,

the white-faced heron gliding to water,
the possum's guileless gaze
claspsing the night-tree;

the growling from the long grass,
skittering to the crevice; the careering
with a leathery buoyancy
through the twilight air;

the running, nodding, twining, trailing,
that is purplish, tall, early, golden,
and what goes white-lipped,
copper-headed, striped —

convinced that my own hand,
making marks this place
thrived without until yesterday
to summon these spirits,

half-sound half-idea, can enchant
the inheritors of terra nullius,
my neighbours, to know
that even though one form
or another of such beauty
can be stamped out
by colonial boots on the ground,
extinguished forever, this
fidelity is untouched, irrepressible.


## The Rainbow Explained

*Urizen...stood in the Human Brain*
*And all its golden porches grew pale with his sickening light.*
— William Blake

On our right as we drive
in the drizzly afternoon
back from Bunnings, a rainbow,
like an errant streak
of impossible paint
on the grey old day,

just beginning to arch as it
vanishes in cloud. My son,
who's 12, and about to finish
Primary School, says
'people must have been amazed.'

'People?'

'Before they knew...'

Around here, not so long ago,
people saw the Rainbow
Serpent rearing.

But how my son responds now
is to marvel
at how those ignorant
others must have marvelled.


## Wonders of the Universe (According to the Celebrity Materialist)

*Our science (like our technics) is maniacal because it bears the
cultural burden of finding meaning for its society where meaning
cannot possibly be found...*
— Theodore Roszak

He goes out into the universe
(well, his instruments do)
looking for answers (well,
his questions are), and is
amazed by the *emptiness*.

But one day, he says,
we will find the Answer out there,
and finding this Answer
is the ultimate quest...

Or he is crouched by the Ganges —
where the great mysteries lean
into our knowing all around
with their animal heads
and profusion of arms —

declaring that if we shrink politely
from Shiva's embrace,
then here we may touch
a greater mystery: *carbon.*


## Station

A tiny movement
in the corner of my eye,
like a migraine flicker,
as I sit in the idling train
before departure,

there again – and I see

it's a twitch of the ice that's formed
up where a column supports
the platform roof with the flat of its hand,
like a pulse on its iron wrist,

the morning's warmth sending
a trickle quickly down
one crooked track,

the exact same squiggle
dashed off faithfully each time
like the flourish
at the end of a signature.

As I watch it keeps happening
like lightning striking in precisely
the same place over and over
from a miniature white sky,

or a micro flash flood,
though this must be
how a mighty river looks
to the sun-god: a timid,
fragile little creature swerving
across open ground to home:

waiting for the brief surge
of new-born water, the image of it
congeals and inverts in my memory
to become the slow squirm upwards
of the moist translucent joey
towards its secluded teat.

As the train prepares to haul us
off to the capital and our working day, this
glimpse of primordial going –

like stillness's fidget,
and the tear it sheds.

## Waking Near the Yarrowee

In the quiet of early morning,
birds are speaking
the language of water.

It can hardly be said that I live
by the river: it passes almost
as close behind as the road
does in front, but
a few more generic houses
stand between me and its slender,
dam-enfeebled, ancient flow,
like fortifications at the border

of suburbia: they are rooves
over our heads, I know,
but the reverent canopy
that would once have shrouded
all of this soft, moist land here
and its shining secret
has been torn aside
to accommodate them...

Swept half a world away
by a tide of migration
from my birthplace on the Humber's
banks of gleaming mud, and deposited
on the dazzling sands of the Swan,
then drawn across the continent by currents
I was told I shouldn't resist, like a rip,
until I came to rest here, my head

lies by the Yarrowee, now,
like a river-stone through which
the water-birds' carolling resonates
as their praise, and as my longing
for the river-world.

## DIY

*it is by not choosing that the object chooses itself within us.*
– Jean Klein

*i*

Not sure if I'm doing it
or the house: the jobs
seem to choose their own moment:

after weeks feeling obstructed,
lethargic, beset by complications,
I find one day that simply to raise my eyes,
let alone my hand, is to begin,
as if I've been properly waiting
for an invitation, not merely stalling.

But then it side-steps my approach,
dismantles my plan, sends me out
to fetch what it needs, or leads me away
to what should come first.

Here I am now crouched
in a corner outside,
in the crook of the house's elbow
where the laundry wall meets
the living room's at right angles —

as if it had strong-armed me here
the way I wrangle my son around
in a faux headlock —

attending to where its skin's been grazed
by Ballarat's seasons playing rough.

*ii*

You know you're in a blind rage,
even while managing
to follow steps laid out
by someone in lucid calm...

And you know,
even as the nail sinks home,
as the shining stripe of paint advances
along the faded old weatherboard,
it's only your misery
you're completing.

What cackhanded, careless rush
has joined you to the physical world
in such a way that your every move
brings it down on your head?

## Bright House

Dislike
of the task:
of your actions as you do it,
of the materials and the tools,
of the time it's taking:

how your house is darkened
by this dislike!

Without it, all of its rooms
could brighten, one after the other,
as you go there — the way they do
as each day turns it in its hand
like an object of perennial wonder —

but with no shadow following...


## Home

I find myself searching
for the innocence of my house,

taking comfort in the relative simplicity
of tin, wood, glass,
that the earth may not have been
too badly torn or poisoned
to contrive my shelter.

And I find myself trying to recognise
the outdoors cold in the indoors cold,
wanting to inhabit
just one breathing space
of the indigenous air, just a nook
in this dark-treed country sloping
and softening towards the creek.

I imagine treading the ground
below the palely glowing platform
of my floorboards, my feet really
knowing where I live…


.


An 'old' house — 'Victorian' —
faded and dog-eared and listing,
but the rough, reddish timbers
of its framework, braced
in the still gloom of the roof
or wall cavity, look
and smell new-cut.

Here I am in this home that feels
like an overcoat too big for me,
hunched like one of the homeless,
watching the parade, mumbling
a rhythmic commentary to myself.

## On the Theft of My New TV

I spent a fair while
choosing where to put it,
lifting it here and there,
arms wide as if to embrace
the long-lost or forgiven,
setting it down carefully
on its one shiny supple flat black foot,
then standing back, taking stock,
eyes roaming and returning to what
would be the most watched place...

But in the end it was passed
out through the bedroom window
by hands unknown, wrapped presumably
in the sheet missing from my bed,
and placed in another house altogether.

And so we sat with Ryokan watching
the moon, until insurance, like good karma
that accumulates by monthly payments
restored a simulacrum of what was taken,
as if nothing had happened.

## Break and Enter

Arriving home, I discovered
that the wind had elbowed its way
through the laundry window,
thin glass and flimsy frame
in pieces on the floor,

and then shouldered aside
the heavy old door to the living room —
thickset sentry of the house's original
rear wall, long since retired —
and swept photographs off shelves,
knocked over the flowers...

After this forced entry and mischief, though,
it hadn't fled, but calmed down and stayed,
sauntering around, mingling
as if invited.


## Shared Care
for Jim

I'd heard of it working ok,
but that machinery
of drop-offs and pick-ups,
of Dad's house and Mum's house
and every other birthday, Christmas,
scared the hell out of me:
what if, when it started up,
it mangled you?

On the first of *my* days, most of me
wasn't breathing for fear you'd
wake up to what was happening,
ask 'why isn't mummy here?'

But what I hadn't factored in
was the part you'd play:
your easy way with circumstance,
your mysterious gearing down

of conflict, smooth transition
to wherever you are, whoever
you're with; as if it was you
who'd designed the whole shebang,
and it was your gentle energy driving it.

Your childhood is a divided land,
across whose rifts and chasms
and turbulence we send you
on ornate little bridges of euphemism:
'Daddy's turn...',
'lucky to have two houses...'

But in either dominion
you are an agent of harmony.

The reconciliation you dream of
cannot be, your bold schemes unworkable:
her barbecue you mention
I could come to, the party
at my place she could help with...

The one roof over us has lifted off
and spun away in the kind of storm
you're still sleeping through, and yet
you've shown us there need not
be ruin, desolation: that a home
may be broken like bread.

And as you take nourishment
everywhere, from everything,
and grow, so does the peace.

## 'Shock and Awe'

My son at that time, when the sky
above the children of Baghdad
began to flash and boom, was five,
and still afraid of storms.
When thunder rumbled he'd run
from his room to ours, a drum-roll
of his small feet across the floor-boards before
the silent finale of his dive through the air
to safety in our bed...

## Leaving the Noise in Peace

*It is not the noise that disturbs you, it is you who disturb the noise!*
– Ajahn Chah

Sleeping-bagged inside our thin-skinned,
translucent house, flimsily sheltered
as if by those ephemeral skeins
of web or gummy dew you find
strung between twigs and leaves in the bush,
the wind that night blew and blew and blew.

We were camped by the Aire River, right next
to the forest, which threshed and roared
without respite. I couldn't sleep,
there seemed an unignorable note
of threat in the noise, and I was worried,
too, that Jim, only seven then,
would be frightened. But in the morning
he said he'd slept like a log.

So clamorous and unrelenting
the wind that night, yet only now
am I beginning to hear it, and to realize
that Jim heard it too, perfectly well.


## Scythe

The grass is never as short, now,
as when the steel hurricane
of the mower had roared over
and flattened it: my unpracticed scything
leaves it lank, glittering as the wind
ruffles it, and no doubt sparkling within
with the *things that creep and flye,*
given the elbow room and cover.
It clings to your step, whispering,
and we feel a little more
like creatures living in the earth's hair
than abstractions on a green plane.

Quiet now, the work is relieved
of that sense of frenzy a howling
machine seizes you with:
I wonder how many of the power-tool
generation have ever heard
the birds sing as they mow,
or heard a metal blade rung faintly
by the grass blades as they yield
(if such hearing went on deepening
might we hear the ringing of the grass
blades as, growing, they slice the air?)

And of course you don't have to share
the tangy, incendiary atmosphere
engines need, or suffer their toxic breath:
the garden's fragrant air alone

is the fuel for your archaic motions,
though the scythe itself has such an oblique
and roundabout way of cutting
that the crouch and swing of my body, the pull
and push of my arms, seem exertions
that commune with it in an occult way,
orders transposed rather than obeyed, as if
neither of us could be quite held responsible.


## Gardening Beyond the Garden
for the Wattle Flats Pootilla Landcare Group

My body bends towards
this ground that isn't mine.

Out here, amongst
the push of life up
from everywhere
that the efforts
of the fences of suburbia
are absurdly end-on to,

the seedling is
almost weightless
in my hand,
squeezed and drawn
from its pod —

as I remember
my new-born son was
when I carried him
for the first time –

a little root-tangle
clinging to a grainy darkness,
but the trunk-strand
strong enough already
to support its outsized
leaf-heads.

In the distance, the buildings
of the town squat
on their bluestone haunches
like Fuseli's demon
on the prone land.


## Autumn Evening, Brown Hill Oval

The light is fading. It's warm,
but we also pass through coolnesses
that remind me of the rooms
on the South side of my house,

though these out here, weirdly
stable as they seem, are not
corralled by walls and ceilings,
but are air being itself, visiting
its ghostly architecture on you.

Our black dog drifts obscurely
between the oval and the forest alongside,
like an ember of the darkness
that will soon engulf us:

we can hardly see
the fluoro tennis ball now,
but the full moon, flattened slightly
as if it's just left the bat,
is getting brighter as it rises.


## The Frogs' Story

After years of searching the little pond's
cavity of idle, cloudy water, finally these dots
with a shred of themselves riffling out behind
like banners in the wind.

It's like that episode in the story
of materialist science, when the hitherto invisible,
guilty microbes were discovered
in their act of infection, squirming
under our magnified, enlightened stare:

which shows you how much
that mode of enquiry,
with its microscopic eye
and crumb of brain, might know.

My relief that the neighbourhood has enough
health left for this to happen is as real
as when I feel my own begin to seep back
after the exhaustion of illness.

My seven year-old's room is closest
to the chirping of the frogs when it starts,
and sitting up in bed he's transfixed
by their arrival in our garden
of their own accord, as if already dreaming:
as if there's no story I could
tell now which would ease him
more wondrously into sleep.


## Pelicans at Lake Burumbeet

We had expected to be looking out over,
not straight up, for the view, as we were
at first, at an expanse of water
choppy and brown, searching the far shore
for anything remarkable a crossing might attain:

there was only an indistinct blandness of paddocks,
with the odd yellow slick of canola, as we stood
frisked ethereally by the wind
for any hidden motives we'd brought.

But as we made our way along the bank,
passing wary anglers whose four-wheel drives
perched gingerly on the spongy ground
they know is taboo for them, several
hefty pelicans drifted down, and then
in a reedy inlet where the water idled glassily
we found a whole mob of them gathered,
manoeuvring amongst each other like those toy cars
that push off automatically from obstacles.

We stayed for a while like peripheral guests
no one takes any notice of, but when
we set off back to our car, one after another
took flight, and followed high above, stopping us
to watch, heads tilted back, their spiral gliding
giving us depth-perception of the sky.

Why this sudden interest? Or were they
making play with this delusion
that we're the centre of everything's attention,

mocking, with their majestic aerial ease,
our earth-bound, two-legged crawling,

surfing the whirlpool rising from our minds to show us
our turbulence even as we think we're being tranquil?

It was as if a sign were being drawn,
over and over, we couldn't decipher…

Were these belated, expansive gestures
of courtesy for our leaving, or a vulture-like,
wheeling pursuit of the doomed?

Whether regal escort or our safe passage
hugely unravelling, our memory of Lake Burumbeet
is of watching, with eyes upraised, dizzied slightly,
the place where no water can settle, and seeing there
a tracery of curving flights, like a soaring, slow clockwork,
like ripple-circles traveling an immaculate smoothness.

# Ground

Yesterday I worked in the garden as the light
withdrew slowly as a tide, taking with it
the forms I was wrangling —
the old gate, wire, star picket —
until my hands, alone in the dark,
seemed to be dreaming them:
smoothness, sharpness,
resistance, yielding...

This morning as I resume
I sit down on the ground,
whose solidity has seemed
dull and endless to me
since I moved inland, far
from the bright crumbling
of earth into ocean
I had always lived next to —

but am surprised by its buoyant
warmth, and the gritty, mineral smell
that's rather like the beach:

as if my ache of exile was nothing more
than my senses' baggage,
while at heart they were always willing
to rejoice in where I am now.

## Mess

Greedy for completion, I nevertheless
drag myself away for lunch,
the materials and implements and debris
of three or four inter-related
jobs glaring at me as I go.

I wonder whether my life
will be in such a mess
when I'm obliged to drift
away from that,

        and as I watch
the lithe black star pickets
basking undriven, the little pile of soil
that has risen, the old gate helpless
on its back, and the power tools
lying in the grass, all shimmering
in the summer afternoon,

I'm suddenly unsure if they amount
to order or disorder,
the unfinished or the finished.


## Hedge

The hedge is bee-loud: a few weeks ago
I was about to trim it, when my son said
not yet, it hasn't blossomed
so the bees would miss out.

Now it's as if the swarm has metamorphosed
into this green wall so it can settle
for a while in suburbia,
in this bland enough form,
though frayed and flower-spangled,
intensely perfumed and buzzing,

and the blackberry shoots arcing out
as if it's springing leaks of a wilder being.

If you go very close the hum becomes
more intense, like a secretive zeal
on the brink of action, and you half expect
to be stung as you brush past,
but just merge harmlessly.

And when we leave in the car
that waits shining but subdued
alongside, its fragrance comes too,
having slipped in as nimbly
and soundlessly as the dog.

The fruit, all this, of my twelve-year-old's
timely advice. Given he's been working with me
through the seasons here for so long now −
admiring their expressions, anticipating their needs,
both of us taking their direction −

it should come as no surprise
that when I raise my shears he responds
on behalf of an unborn plenitude,
with a gently earnest voice that wakes me
to where I really am,
and where my duty lies…

## Holding Water

*We say amiss*
*This or that is:*
*Thy word is all, if we could spell.*
— George Herbert

The water shows my bird bath's
out of true, slid to one side
like a dislocated lens
in a stone eye; shows also

that it's not held, actually, by that vessel:
a shard of it appears to be, yes,
but only as the flow of the wind
seems to be held as a keening note
by the edge of a building:

It is held, we might say, by gravity,
but when you inspect the dynamics
of that explanation, you find a machine
without an engine, an angel-shaped
absence at its heart, as if
there's something there but to the old science
it will always be a blurry nothing, fixed
as its focus is on the material.

And when you look more closely
at water itself, the perfect line
its surface is supposed to keep
bulges with tension; or if you
draw back from it so far
that you can see the blue droplet

of the planet whole, with the grains
of continents afloat in it, then water's
preparedness to curve and enfold
confounds any cold geometrical
image you may have had of it.

What is going on, then, as it surges back,
by routes we revere as beneficent
or bewail as disastrous, to the level
of its greatest gathering, always
with an unerring efficiency you'd think
could only be born of the lucidity of indifference?
Where does the truth of water lie?

This little shining pool of it
I've corralled here for the birds
manifests the answer as perfectly
as those grander, tumultuous events:

though wedged lop-sidedly
in a coarse and a grimy setting,
it remains the flawless jewel
of its own and all existing things' desire

for return: for rest from existence
in the heart of pure Being.